THE
INSTALLATION
OF
FEAR

Also by Jon Curley

POETRY

New Shadows (2009)

Angles of Incidents (2012)

Hybrid Moments (2015)

Scorch Marks (2017)

Remnant Halo (2021)

CRITICISM

Poets and Partitions: Confronting Communal Identities in
Northern Ireland

The Poetry and Poetics of Michael Heller: A Nomad Memory
(Co-Editor with Burt Kimmelman)

Events and Victims by Bartolomeo Vanzetti (Editor)

THE INSTALLATION OF FEAR

JON CURLEY

MARSH HAWK PRESS

East Rockaway, New York • 2025

Marsh Hawk books are published by Marsh Hawk Press, Inc., a not-for-profit corpora-
tion under section 501(c)3 United States Internal Revenue Code.

Cover photograph: Jon Curley

Cover and book design: Hedi Allameh; copyright © Hedi Allameh 2025

Publication of this book was supported by a generous grant from the Council of Liter-
ary Magazines and Presses via the New York State Council of the Arts.

Library of Congress Cataloging-in-Publication Data

Names: Curley, Jon, author.

Title: The installation of fear / Jon Curley.

Description: First edition. | East Rockaway, New York : Marsh Hawk Press, Inc., 2025.

Identifiers: LCCN 2024023729 | ISBN 9798987617700 (paperback)

Subjects: LCGFT: Poetry.

Classification: LCC PS3603.U755 I57 2025 | DDC 813/.6--dc23/eng/20240524

LC record available at https://lccn.loc.gov/2024023729

M Marsh
H Hawk
P Press

Marsh Hawk Press
P.O. Box 206
East Rockaway, New York 11518-0206
www.marshhawkpress.org

ACKNOWLEDGEMENTS

Deep gratitude & beatitude to all my family, friends, students, collaborators, and co-conspirators.

Special thanks to Derek Coyle & Dan Morris.

This volume is dedicated to the Future.

One need not be a Chamber—to be Haunted—
One need not be a House—
The Brain has Corridors—surpassing
Material Place—

Emily Dickinson

The festival will begin
in filth and fear

The stars will fall
When death approaches.

Georges Bataille

I have at times wanted and wished for time
to stand still at a particular certain moment.
If it would all stay this way this would be
heaven, but of course (reality) the other side
of the whole soon reappears. Things are never
constant. Disaster is coming. Disasters are coming.

Sonny Rollins

TABLE OF CONTENTS:

Regarding The Installation of Fear—

Dateline: Now

Consider the globe as a vast teeming gallery, an exhibition (think JG Ballard's phrase "atrocity exhibition"—the phrase, though not his eponymous short story), an exhibition filled with physical structures that are emblematic installations, actual artworks of the misbegotten machinery of misery we have placed like landmines over the expanse and in our minds, our minds' mines. So physical structures and mental structures imitate each other, become physical and mental strictures, generate fear and so many other disquieting, even terrifying sentiments and sediments. Fear and Terror as structures, as styles, a doom idiom, informing the Estate of the Real, Real Estate.

Herein is a survey of that landscape, that mindscape, sometimes seemingly clinical, deceptively detached, apparently objective, impishly impersonal— but also serving as a negative archive of a new vision, a catalog raisonné for a redeemed image of this globe, to be conceptualized as a work-in-progress towards a tentative hope, a provisional possibility, an otherworld within the confines of this one. In the place where fear was installed some different structure might be placed, closing the show that was darkness (invincible?), traumatically contemporary, most certainly here. And now.

THE
INSTALLATION
OF
FEAR

The Installation of Fear

Sum of the parts, some of the parts

were invoiced, intoned. All those invoices

dwelling as opposed to in-dwelling. Waiting.

The machinery confers a kind of hope of/for

obliteration, the embedded conceit, crypto-

concrete, of the technological urge. Age.

Agape, estranged, all pixilated into hazardry

("obsolete" in any sense, especially the non-).

The Installation of Fear is a mixed-media

marvel of materials locally and internationally

sour(c)ed, stretched canvases of bodies, flesh

really (really!), combined and curated

by the Orders of Gen-eration & Gen-ocide

(and so on and so forth and ever again, ever

again, never-ending, always reliably rot).

Abstract and not, the figures dot the lines

like red blood cells or the cells in which blood

reddens to a burst of grave, floating in the…

ether, virtual sphere, virtue-less here, air

suffocating into the emblem of artful or artless

execution, brush, palette, & firing squad.

Glock & roll, lo & behold, don't count

your hatchets or hatchlings before they match.

The artists who did this, did us. Us was those.

Us brought here by our corporate sponsors, benefactors,

benzene benisons of the famed, famished, & further

gone, ghosted by the headlines obscuring the art.

But the exhibition is now on view regardless:

Inlaid finally now, the final virtual painted stone.

Free now for fear (the paint has pain in it, fear an ear).

Be afraid. Be very afraid. All has been installed and ill-
willed for a while. Chaste, seemingly, those Claimants who

no longer claim to possess, but only show forth the
penumbra of our Commonwealth Commons, innocent in
their neo-sylvan styles of post-brutalist Terror.

Interrogation

Always logos treats us as if
the pain would not show;

I cannot prepare a portfolio
of the pain you will know

(though its variants are clearly
accosting, dearly costing).

Why does the sliver usually
follow the shimmer?

Were we asked to ache
besides the pleasantries or before?

Some grievances are better
to bear than to bury—

When I seem to succumb
to the solace of any possible solution

I will then change the equation,
inelegantly wreck all and any futile fortunes.
Call it the craft of catastrophe, controlled

accident, honest indignity, fate's annuity.

Elsewhere little more fair peering
into the panorama peopled thus:

Quietly she/he/they quaked
in still lives, lives climatically forsook,

still alive but inert. May the mental currency
convert most industries to invisibilities

& may some of us mine the depths
over a prayer's precipice.

Now that there is no longer time to talk,
  I am asking that you relent a little
while we await the evitable outcome
  not so much declared as assumed
as we peer amid the gossamer-y gloom
  of conceivable furtherance into
the realm beyond the wound wound
  like a bandage staunching that wound
from the war that was, hoped for by
  a staunch supporter of your war wounds:
the resident enemy that is your ally always:
  Only.

Strafed by wraiths in the course of escape

(in the corner of escape)

Cemented in disgrace by constructed space

Renovated renderings of any place downstreet from grace

No need to nurture gentrification or any other place

I am not in place or peace or set to see space as peace-place

Whether or not the weather actually surrounds this face

set to look out across the planes, plans, scales, shales,

shoals, holes, coals (cooling), is predicated on a sense

of scene that may no longer have meaning, as leaving,

as in, meaning has been leaving, has been moving from here,

this scene, this insubstantial grid gotten by dishonest gardeners

(really, undevelopers), ever since we/they uprooted the

earth to build upon in exchange for the worth to profit upon.

And whatever contest is convened about the ethereal

versus the material, the vacant lot or the virtuous spot,

a semblance of self and place, that higher, better built-scene

will come to haunt us. It comes to haunt us as we arrive

where we began: to build and grow, hoe and hasten,

under the sign of the state and its ignoble fate, the state

of wrath, and those wraiths that strafe: fierce foundation

forces for locations achieved through the unreal

logic of the real estate of our unreal optics or

unrealized expectations. Once there was a Great Refusal

for this Haunting Housing Development (HHD) but

we cannot find it now/forever: No ground to give.

At the Brink

Or maybe the threshold, however this arrival works
when all is still, when all is still struck, now past
that confounding gate, here is reached the condition
of anomaly thereby maybe we can pass. The conditionals
are relentless, appalling, keep us supposing
direction is elevation—but the night (nigh) is still
calling. I address you somehow over these terms
and dimming of lights, honestly confounded (still)
but bracing for embrace, imminent must it be,
because I cherish not only this art but the space
where dwells it and the heart of its governance. Gain
please this domain where we might instill lights
in the arctic, in the attic, in the antithesis of arranged
formats. This is a plea, a visioning, a wreck-oning.

Strive for the syntax of renewal—
that thought imbued before concussed.
I trip over tropes and fail to conceive
structures that might undue this harm,
this four alarm fire fake-out. Arson
takes its toll, acid eats the columns
that upraised (or might have) hopes.
Signifiers saturated, cleaving to cladding,
won't offer enough word to gird the need.
When I strove for that renewal syntax
function and form, I did so also at witness
to the storm and was broken up before
I could reach the shore of that thought.

Again.

the syntax of grace
                the syntax of grief—
I parsed a part
                between the two
& still I found myself
                between, amid, through
& against the two: grace/grief:
                what is the space between
the two? the me of you?
                the who of you?

Everywhere ears
    stuffed nightly

those fears

agon arrested then
    seared

So many securities
    scorned by those sounds
of imminent surrender or
    sedition, to the melody
of murder or perjury or disgrace

Enveloped in that diabolical
    acoustic encasement is still
the bleat of sheep-song, those who
    confound a shepherd's order
with the herd instinct of trust,
    of traversing greener pastures
where no pecking orders settle
    and a new green sound is heard.

Impact Statement

ardent inquiry
  reliquary
choice sub-set
  strung lines
splayed limbs
  bollixed box-set
archives agitated
  sealed sections
rotted renditions
  elliptical indentations
forced rhythms
  evidence of torture
tortured evidence
  the undersigned acknowledging
great granted legislations
  of Terror patented
in the great persecutions
  equated with the prevarications
endowed with no deliberation
  conscious concession to
Hell heaven-sent by
  legatees of mayhem
stretched across the wastes:
  wastes of land, wastes of world

all the words abased by
  daily devotions to distraction
inaction, the fracture of
  a thousand minds mazed
in the trough of tough times
  and yet, as read today—
"E quindi uscimmo a riveder le stelle"
Or translated into I-talian:
  "And so we came forth, and once
again beheld the stars." Amen.

Poem for Bob Thompson (1937-1966)

Painter premier, quester art star (after the fact
and facts and art go together weirdly like your
Edenic scenes where strange vicious birds enter
the scenes and disturb them. Inter them.):

Let me come at you multiply in various modes,
off-kilter, and out to sea because, you see,
when you left the palette for the paper
you gave some navigation charts as to where
you watery were…

You wrote in thick, riverine ink:

I'm awake
I'm awake

I'm a wave licking
The shore—

My tongue is
water bathing
my lips

My eyes struggle to see the
bathing of my lips

I ...

My tongue is
                Me

In your wake I take the fifth take
of, intake of, that arresting orange canvas
of yours as it comes crashing down
amid my mind's stretched sense
of all that comes down the pike and wakes;
all that that made your figures fret among
those aerial Leviathans, those bane birds.

What was your Leviathan specifically, Bob?
Bopping as you did among the painted fields
and selves and seas, you were there too with
George Oppen: Truth is also the pursuit of it.

The two shows of yours I attended last month made
some advertising overtures for your work, neither
of which you would have perhaps written or painted
but let them fold into this poem-portrait and see where
they lead:

So let us all be citizens

&

Agony & Ecstasy

Some allowed to be more than others, "those" citizens (who?)
while the ratio of 'A' to 'E' is always in favor of the former:
An Agony. As Now. As Then. As the poem, "An Agony. As Now,"
written by Leroi Jones whose family you painted. That family
is us and ours, maybe. Like your work, *Truth is also the pursuit.*
of it.

Set-Pieces

1.

Cries
    Crisis of Cries
Crises of Conscience
      Not consubstantial with science
Cons conversant with our Condition
      Then Chorus of Code

2.

Transitive light
  Transcribe light
As ever
  (that is an order; an order of pattern
misrecognition & misdirection)

3.

All too many paths obstructed

Terror in the grid-lit imperium

Pleroma flecked with grease

Designs of cruelty/Notes of futility

4.

The iconic is a Claw
Absent this icon is the irenic
Anti-ruin as against oblivion

Sage presage reprieve
No return save to pre-salvation
opposite the non-renewable
adjacent to the inevitable yet
balanced there with the possible

5.

Explosion—and then: ....

                    ....Expulsion
                              (though not extinction)

erasures enveloping
markings—secreted language
languishing, waiting to be broken

or brokered

a new script

or then silence

6.

The residence of resistance

The residue of If

Beckettian Semi-Reversal

From things about to reappear,
I turn toward, not away—the fear
that I will lose them when I miss them
is the force that garners grace. And saves.

ex speCters

Quest narratives abound with such fecundities—
the waved hand and woven heart, the spirit gliding
across the departing arc, a resplendent invocation
of intercessional occupation, the signal foray
into miracle's destiny, fate's nemesis.

Are you now cemented or semaphored,
folded or fjorded? Now, in the green grip
of goner logic? You have to decide which
impasse will be settled and what way you
shall move on spirit-ships resembling
Erebus and Terror according to your "wish."

crimes flung like allelujahs
over their carcasses now canvases

Fragment for what was meant
for a fossil
that was
meant for me

Red rhymes in the green syntax of abasement
still manage to arrange a pattern into a pocket
into which the stitch of subjugation is frayed
ever so slightly in a sentence not eternally ached

Haunted, had it,
catch, release

Laments nourished in the sprawling space, those echo-
chants trembling in the aftermath of so many death-
masks worn in the habit of scars, SARS, scares. No stars,
just steles.

immiserated immigrants: submersible titans: oceanic eeries:
mass mythology of mayhem and in spite still reveries,
oxidizing conceits swim past hopeless bruised buoys,
destinies plumb depths reverse engineering drowning
hopes with utopic maybes of tomorrow tides

rigor mortis de rigueur, default spiritual mode
made dominant in the mental lockdown invoked
by code of processed processionals of congregants
bent to find astonishment at the unfastening of it All

Even despite agonies, engulfing calamities,
and the seeming passion for ruination
(and ruins?) (t)here engenders angels
at angles secular and secure in the science
of resistance and the seduction of dissent.

Acquiescence to 'evil' in the empirical sense:
a convention by us in almost every occasion
where the term moves from the theological
to the textbook logical in the complicit bindings
of the book you now have in your hands.

Wish fulfillment and/or dream fantasy:
Those coniferous trees grow carnivorous
leaves that leach the life of lackluster hunters
armed with Uzi guards in their secret jacuzzis
and plant the seed of destruction for any non-
naturalist destroyers who, in turn, become
voyeurs of their own imminent erasures

A phoenix cannot rise more than a few times
in a millennium; so for the temperature to rise
so high in Phoenix these past weeks shows
that Promethean fire was a kind of fracking
before the score. Weather as abjection:
inner and outer, what we are and what we
are to be abhorred. The weather vane
charts a bleak ontology of meteorology.

Sculpt a skepticism and behold how it embeds
the weight of futility in its wake. Be vigilant
for varieties of non-indignant artifacts either
indigenously blessed or potentially produced.
Art-making is not the cure but a procedure
to yield faith-giving forms.

Blasted heaths and institutions, perverse those
universities given over to death-dealing instructions;
healing is not only a process or state but a destination
amid the lifeless landscapes, a thicket-ing/thickening
plot of relentless creation. A forcefield of content
set to bloom rather than shatter, to shelter, make
or mend better.

Law of the excluded middle: if the barren binary
is left to wither, translate the trans into a stance
with better semblance. For they who are many
are mostly you and I and We and They. Go
(re-) figure.

A special dispensation: civil discord is discarded
but only with the demise of the iron boot
and Right angle geometry that merges an image
of genocide with fasces-formed fraternity. Other-
wise, no truce with the furies, the fascists, or complicits.

Among the missed opportunities that were once my friends:
"solidarity," "revelation," & "transformation":
I send this signal in both enlightened envelope
& light beam to you—which is to say 'me,'
which was only ever us all anyhow.

On myriad screens, the vapid or void-vectoring condition—
on the horizon, manifold canopies & verdant vistas
that conspire to hasten occasions of true technological
know-how: that is, the green scene short-circuiting
the audacity of the risible, non-rhizomatic zombie
action of cursors, keyboards, and nets—inter,
outer, & otherwise.

The fragrance of fragments, the aroma of the ever-incomplete—
of these I seek in the wake of finished forms that finalized
the lifeless life that ever seemed the direst sign of retreat.

Ever supported by the ever departed, the endgame advocates
fantasized our extinctions and inserted infections into
our ears, minds, and wombs while calling it salvation.
The infection was their hatred and their liturgy became Law.

Incongruously, the incognito bogeyman laid down
their guns only after hastening the hostage-taking
of our freedom with a brisk bullet to the brain:
ours thus dead, theirs deader. The lead poisoning
moved ardently wound to wound with an amendment
as irritant, not solvent. Armed but mind-less.

Affixed wretchedly in space, the Great Limiter
eyeing us as we try to gather any available graces
for us to go on. Geometries of tyrannies pit expanse,
regenerating their forms from that point to that history.

Climate correctives issued in words wind through
the channels and platforms, provoking distress signals
like barely moving weather vanes. Under canopies
of darkening trees, strange animals stare in the breeze.

Despite, perhaps because, sweeping sheets of panic there still arises some static of solace, the clarifying conductor of creation rising above the station of what is. Recourse to invention, entrenchment, protest against entombment, modest faith in the traffic of marvels.

A cottage industry of cruelty permeates precincts where we
fastened, now fester in. Inscrutable, those agents glued to their devices
aligned with surveillance and scrutiny, their personalities
pulling away from their bodies, flesh mimicries cancelling
organic matter, impersonating human form while placing
persons in lock-ups, chokeholds, standard-issue identity boxes.
Calendar check: four summers ago a wake-up call; now,
resistant spirit thrives in hives of isolation, near zones of
contamination. Indoctrination? Please place containers
of amnesia and aphasia here and here, then and now.

Unvarnished expression would command confession
to evade the unseemly fact of the anti-matter that I
present not a presence but an absence in a stanza
stolen from Anonymous with all credit due to you.

Who shall sit for the silhouette while the shadow
outlines a sensibility encased within the idea
of a fleshed-out portrait of an x-rayed essence?

Forever conflating lesions with lessons,
hemorrhages with homilies,
these verse-surgeons sound songs
of scarred, stunted states and mis-diagnose
the malady that has transformed anthem
to antithesis: dirge ditty of anti-liberty
libertarian non-lyric. Panacea? *Populismo!*

Darker is the light by which we signal site—
the steps of which beckon our ascent to
the unsteady staircase to lyric's labyrinth
through stanzas thickly settled by unsettling
subjects ready to engender their entrenchments
over enchantments for those who would really
wish to sing, shatter, swerve, and sway.

I am not what word you see.
You see? Dictionary desert
of lo-fi heaving estuary
of emotion. Can we still be
Ends?

All the emended tendencies moved murder right back to the margins, mirroring the motion of white-out erasures of any real narratives heretofore hatched. Premium truth is uncouth to the ones who should be replaced, displaced, defaced. De-faced: they already have been (see above), lacking any particularity except the precision of their plans— to undermine, usurp, debase, afflict; vanishing DEI in a cover-up cosmetic retractive act of uncivil rights right before (y)our unseeing eyes.

While the world washed up on the world, the oceans disobeyed gravity and rose from their depths into skies now oceanic, occasionally leaking saline tear drops back to landmasses, both a natural occurrence and a natural gesture of emotional farewell to wasted, wounded things.

Tension becomes the occasion, the invasion a situation
so dependably vile that most witnesses reliably ignore it
and then alleviate any of those tensions with the mention
of invasion with the caveat "if we cannot stop this incursion"
and then quotations are followed by ellipses then joined
comradely by that commonplace veer syndrome that sets us
again off course to find an occasion of tension with the
invasion of—

On the darkling plain: midnight mass graves of penitents
seeking shelter and relief, beatitude not desuetude, not
a nightmare vision or fever dream but the relentless course
of natural progression this third decade of the 21st century
as witnessed regularly by those who have not misplaced
their vision of this vision as those coffins accumulate
as necro-grade ellipses moving across, across, ever across…

No dark without dialectic, a delicate overturning
of those malignant powers pressing against us
framed by the force of reckoning ways not just
out but beyond, searching for salves in and out
of the poem. Deeper into the poem. Seek, Seeker,
deep, deeper into the poem. In its body bodes
the only organ able to fire the neurons against
negation: in the body of the poem of the body
of the poem of the body of the poem of the body

From here—the cynical cynosure beckons compliance—
From there—some residual comeuppance flees despair—
Elsewhere, there are riddles inscribed in dusty documents
awaiting possible translation. What compositions or
coordinates could be construed are not yet for us made
legible but we await a clearing of air, word, and path...

Forensics request:

Please approve the immediate resurrection for this wish
emerging from the festering scrofulous situation to
move from mental abstraction to physical embodiment
and supplement all diets of prayers with the logic
of unimpeded poly-ethical potential: Metaphysics
bleached with blood, practice, contingency, hope-
dash, splash of realism drenched with counter-realism.

Now that we are here together on this page, may I
conjure with you some war and waltz-inspired attitudes
and suggest we dance the death of war with ardor
aerated with the replenishing sublimes of characteristics
unaccustomed to our times. Thus we convey or contrive
a manifesto of a different ego, a differing time, some thrust
from the inadequately usual to the emphatic, not yet-articulated
must (hint: the secret of this trend is no ruse; it can be found
in the scripture of Emily, Audre, Diane, Sonia, Eileen,
and some other scintillating Sister-Poets with worlds
and whirlwinds to invent, augment, widen, and re-wonder).

Sorry to be didactic but there lies the hard work to be had
to acknowledge the encroaching disaster and the enveloping
redemption to inspire either/both dread and/or desire, ice and fire,
curses or amens, revelation of imperative or, alas, the distraught
of no more navigable means (what say you, convened cartographers?).

Then such profusion: a riot of green permeating
once desiccated planes and scenes. Another root
riddled in the hope-converted mind lets grow
a quickening chorus of voices vindicating the verdant
permission of re-building despite ravages & wreckages.

Emblematic of the crisis was the Confederate onslaught, the ripening of hostilities into open, unrelenting agendas: seepage of brain matter polluting all altars under auspices of acts not exactly mandated by State but manufactured by it.

I sense you starving in that approximate place
for the nourishment of authentic exile not press-
ganged into the conforming, middling misery
of standing apart yet not yet quite reaching
that condition of outer space riven with risk.
Continue to think your escape artist-antics
into true detachment like the ecstatic
clairvoyance of the damned yet delivered

Often now, the sense that to resurrect those misguided actions was not misguided at all. Actionable all. Taken, as fierce, vatic enterprises, they consign any cynicism to a very narrow crypt. I credit my friend Elena for reinforcing this truth and un-burying me from a nether-space that would have made me imaginatively, conceptually, dead on idea arrival. I, from her, resist that living death. Amen for solidarity, for commonwealth.

Who do you look for to look out for you, "coreligionist"?

To penetrate the Now is akin to fleeing the circle-
seeming sensation of being on a wheel of fire
and being borne relentlessly into that heap of hurt.
Again. Aghast. A rehearsal for the imagined assembly
of caregivers coming to their/our aid, no longer
dithering, dissembling, overriding the concern
for corrected attitude, for unrestrained adornment
of that ferocious re-figuring of handling how
we move from mere piety and prison to
release and a kind of redemption (not to be
too confused in my messaging of Muses
and Messengers, no matter how either treats us
or are treated by us): Tractatus of supposition
following or during the scattering of us into Dust.

All this offering knelt and spilled down
through and across our/selves, our almost
shrouds, dog us with patterns we can barely
contain or costume without shame or the shelter
of a similar sense. Fixation on the holy or hyper-
real is really a diadem of other new (read: false)
diadems. May we attend/attain succor in lines/lives
outside of these demanding domains (whether
calling them stanzas or penitentiaries, liberation
zones or overrides of our usual moans). Whatever
the ca(u)se, let us not pause, relent, return.

Though the arch agnostic well knows that fate
will attend as moss and morse in the grave—
it shall too become template still for some
ungovernable state. Keep your wits without you
or else keep conduct unprepared for; not
known will be the order of the other day,
the next one, the one beyond, beyond all doors.

So we find us now here, in this habitat,
baked in good riddance, little sense, much less
anything else but abandonment and abeyance,
abject obedience, meager conveyance into
what had seemed a stable structure of meaning
if not feeling: alas, we find (once or once again)
this sentiment a judgement, a call for adjournment:
and we cannot figure out if it is "for" Us or "about" Us.

Despite the strictures, I commit to you,
an envious archetype out of the Blue, into
and beyond it (the Blue). Even as escape
excites possibility, (I) am disarmed, disrobed,
defeated; adversaries surround. No matter:
I cling to the azure awe invested in you
and climb to it (you) and through it. These
prepositions try to chase me, even chasten me,
but I stay stalwart with you wherever I
can find you; confound me, and find deep
Blue sea analogues to envelope me/we.

I am zoning in, zoning out, not knowing whether
what is seen in the scene is terra firma, quicksand,
calenture, abyss, or other. My willed brother, Hölderlin,
grown mad or bold (or both) wrote that he was heading
"To the site and the warning." I am at that site,
I hear the warning, and am in the zone. His lines
come from a poem called "The Poet's Courage."
Not the courage or a site for it can I claim, wresting
counterfeit coordinates from a threadbare figure
I will call a Poet. Still, not getting anywhere...
Anywhere. Just this place, at least for no(w).

Of all the fallen or departed persons kept
legend in memory's grasp, the awe that
arrives with remembrance of the flaws
that never sapped their special-ness
seems to me the apex of miracle-ness
& bids quick reset of ontology & the non-
sense of considered selves, mine/ours/theirs.

Amen.

Given the gift, the quest, the re-
quest—could the contract
among the contrite be
rendered real, authentic, true?

Promissory notes on promontory faults?

Our population now decries covenants
or commons, instead opts for
borrowed optics, AIs, kill calipers,
radio raptors, sexy sadism.

But perhaps there is delivery
from the deleterious, delirious,
demented, & "dead"?

>>> In that envelope is
the solution & mystery
for much of what is here
& much what we need.

Rip it open, ripen the moment.

Coda

Never foregone or forgotten

All the vestiges of vital words
after being casketed & shunned
emerged like specters
from materialist
malevolent constraints
and withered all those skins
like enemies contained
at least temporarily by
the method of magical
rethinking—

(Here, the poem and you break
down, break apart, become
such new selves: but which?)

—begin anew!
            —Or not!
                        —Or now!

Notes

The italicized lines of poetry in "Poem for Bob Thompson" were transcribed from a display case accompanying the exhibition "Bob Thompson: Agony & Ecstasy" (April 1-July 7, 2023) at Michael Rosenfeld Gallery in Manhattan.

Some of these poems appear in the Fall 2024 issue of the *Marsh Hawk Review.*

About the Author:

Jon Curley is the author of *Remnant Halo* (2021), *Scorch Marks* (2017), *Hybrid Moments* (2015), *Angles of Incidents* (2012), and *New Shadows* (2009). He teaches in the Humanities and Social Sciences Department of New Jersey Institute of Technology in Amiri Baraka's New Ark, New Jersey. He now lives in New York City.

Visit his website at: www.joncurley.com

Titles From Marsh Hawk Press

Jane Augustine *Arbor Vitae; Krazy; Night Lights; A Woman's Guide to Mountain Climbing*

Tom Beckett *Dipstick (Diptych)*

Sigman Byrd *Under the Wanderer's Star*

Patricia Carlin: *Original Green; Quantum Jitters; Second Nature*

Claudia Carlson *The Elephant House; My Chocolate Sarcophagus; Pocket Park*

Meredith Cole *Miniatures*

Jon Curley *Hybrid Moments; Scorch Marks*

Neil de la Flor *Almost Dorothy; An Elephant's Memory of Blizzards*

Chard deNiord *Sharp Golden Thorn*

Sharon Dolin *Serious Pink*

Steve Fellner *Blind Date with Cavafy; The Weary World Rejoices*

Thomas Fink *Selected Poems & Poetic Series; Joyride; Peace Conference; Clarity and Other Poems; After Taxes; Gossip*

Thomas Fink and Maya D. Mason *A Pageant for Every Addiction*

Norman Finkelstein *Inside the Ghost Factory; Passing Over*

Edward Foster *A Looking-Glass for Traytors; The Beginning of Sorrows; Dire Straits; Mahrem: Things Men Should Do for Men; Sewing the Wind; What He Ought to Know*

Paolo Javier *The Feeling is Actual*

Burt Kimmelman *Abandoned Angel; Somehow*

Burt Kimmelman and Fred Caruso *The Pond at Cape May Point*

Basil King *Disparate Beasts: Basil King's Beastiary, Part Two; 77 Beasts; Disparate Beasts; Mirage; The Spoken Word/The Painted Hand from Learning to Draw/A History*

Martha King *Imperfect Fit*

Phillip Lopate *At the End of the Day: Selected Poems and An Introductory Essay*

Mary Mackey *Breaking the Fever; The Jaguars That Prowl Our Dreams; Sugar Zone; Travelers With No Ticket Home*

Jason McCall *Dear Hero,*

Sandy McIntosh *The After-Death History of My Mother; Between Earth and Sky; Cemetery Chess; Ernesta, in the Style of the Flamenco; Forty-Nine Guaranteed Ways to Escape Death; A Hole In the Ocean; Lesser Lights; Obsessional*

Stephen Paul Miller *Any Lie You Tell Will Be the Truth; The Bee Flies in May; Fort Dad; Skinny Eighth Avenue; There's Only One God and You're Not It*

Daniel Morris *Blue Poles; Bryce Passage;*

Hit Play; If Not for the Courage

Gail Newman *Blood Memory*

Geoffrey O'Brien *Where Did Poetry Come From; The Blue Hill*

Sharon Olinka *The Good City*

Christina Olivares *No Map of the Earth Includes Stars*

Justin Petropoulos *Eminent Domain*

Paul Pines *Charlotte Songs; Divine Madness; Gathering Sparks; Last Call at the Tin Palace*

Jacquelyn Pope *Watermark*

George Quasha *Things Done for Themselves*

Karin Randolph *Either She Was*

Rochelle Ratner *Balancing Acts; Ben Casey Days; House and Home*

Michael Rerick *In Ways Impossible to Fold*

Corrine Robins *Facing It; One Thousand Years; Today's Menu*

Eileen R. Tabios *The Connoisseur of Alleys; I Take Thee, English, for My Beloved; The In(ter)vention of the Hay(na)ku; The Light Sang as It Left Your Eyes; Reproductions of the Empty Flagpole; Sun Stigmata; The Thorn Rosary*

Eileen R. Tabios and j/j hastain *The Relational Elations of Orphaned Algebra*

Susan Terris *Familiar Tense; Ghost of Yesterday; Natural Defenses*

Lynne Thompson *Fretwork*

Madeline Tiger *Birds of Sorrow and Joy*

Tana Jean Welch *Latest Volcano*

Harriet Zinnes: *Drawing on the Wall; Light Light or the Curvature of the Earth; New and Selected Poems; Weather is Whether; Whither Nonstopping*

Tony Trigilio: *Proof Something Happened*

YEAR	AUTHOR	TITLE	JUDGE
2004	Jacquelyn Pope	*Watermark*	Marie Ponsot
2005	Sigman Byrd	*Under the Wanderer's Star*	Gerald Stern
2006	Steve Fellner	*Blind Date with Cavafy*	Denise Duhamel
2007	Karin Randolph	*Either She Was*	David Shapiro
2008	Michael Rerick	*In Ways Impossible to Fold*	Thylias Moss
2009	Neil de la Flor	*Almost Dorothy*	Forrest Gander
2010	Justin Petropoulos	*Eminent Domain*	Anne Waldman
2011	Meredith Cole	*Miniatures*	Alicia Ostriker
2012	Jason McCall	*Dear Hero,*	Cornelius Eady
2013	Tom Beckett	*Dipstick (Diptych)*	Charles Bernstein
2014	Christina Olivares	*No Map of the Earth Includes Stars*	Brenda Hillman
2015	Tana Jean Welch	*Latest Volcano*	Stephanie Strickland
2016	Robert Gibb	*After*	Mark Doty
2017	Geoffrey O'Brien	*The Blue Hill*	Meena Alexander
2018	Lynne Thompson	*Fretwork*	Jane Hirshfield
2019	Gail Newman	*Blood Memory*	Marge Piercy
2020	Tony Trigilio	*Proof Something Happened*	Susan Howe

92